Favourite Classic
COMPOSERS

LIZ GOGERLY

WAYLAND

© Copyright 2004 Wayland

Editor: Hayley Leach
Design: Peter Bailey for Proof Books
Cover design: Wayland
Consultant: Roger Thomas

Published in Great Britain in 2004 by Hodder Wayland,
an imprint of Hodder Children's Books.

This paperback edition published in 2007 by Wayland,
an imprint of Hachette Children's Books.

British Library Cataloguing in Publication Data
Gogerly, Liz
Favourite classic composers
1. Composers – Biography – Juvenile literature
I. Title
780.9'22

ISBN: 9780750252935

Cover: Portrait of Ludwig van Beethoven by Josef Karl Stieler

Picture Acknowledgements
Cover and page 12 Archivo Iconografico, S.A./CORBIS; 4 Bettmann/CORBIS;
6 Archivo Iconografico, S.A./CORBIS; 8 Archivo Iconografico, S.A./CORBIS;
Title page and 10 Bettmann/CORBIS;14 Archivo Iconografico, S.A./CORBIS;
16 Bettmann/CORBIS; 18 Bettmann/CORBIS; 20 Hulton-Deutsch
Collection/CORBIS.

Printed in China

Hachette Children's Books
338 Euston Road
London NW1 3BH

Terms explained in the glossary have been printed in **bold** throughout the text.

Contents

Antonio Vivaldi | 1678-1741

The seventeenth century Italian composer Vivaldi was not well known until quite recently. The man who brought us *The Four Seasons*, perhaps one of the most popular pieces of classical music of all time, was virtually forgotten until the 1920s.

Antonio Lucio Vivaldi was born in Venice (now in Italy) in about 1678. Music was in his blood from an early age. His father was a talented violinist at Venice's St Mark's cathedral. He taught his son to play the violin and insisted upon extra lessons. By the time Vivaldi was 13 he could stand in for his father as a violinist at the cathedral. At 15 his life looked set to take a different path to music when he began training for the priesthood. Though he qualified to become a priest he gave up his religious career in his early twenties due to ill health.

In 1703 Vivaldi became the chief violinist at the Conservatorio dell' Ospedale della Pietà, a respected musical school for orphaned girls.

He worked at the Conservatorio on and off for most of his life. In between times he could be found entertaining Europe's royalty and leading statesmen. When he wasn't playing he

'Venice and Vivaldi, the two words are closely linked in the mind but Venice is a curiosity, magical and ghostly, a jewelled and fantastic relic, while Vivaldi's music is vibrant, surging with life and energy, as passionate and compelling as when it first echoed in the city of the sea.'

Vivaldi (The Illustrated Lives of the Great Composers) by John Booth (Omnibus Press, 1989)

was composing operas and orchestral music. Sadly, by the 1730s Vivaldi's music was going out of fashion and he fell out with the religious leaders of Venice. In 1738 his connection with the Conservatorio was severed and he left his beloved Venice for Vienna in Austria. He hoped to seek a post at the Austrian royal court but unfortunately he was no longer in favour. When he died the following year he was penniless and had to be buried in a pauper's grave.

With Vivaldi's death came years of obscurity. His music was hidden away until 1922 when a huge stash of his work was found in an Italian monastery. In 1939 his music was published and performed for the first time in over two hundred years.

Questions

Why is *The Four Seasons* so special?

A large part of Vivaldi's work is for stringed instruments. *The Four Seasons* has become one of the most popular pieces for any professional violinist to master as it has many violin solos. *The Four Seasons* is important because it is an early example of programme music. This is a composition that follows a theme and describes events or objects, rather like a musical poem. In this particular piece Vivaldi cleverly uses different tempos and arrangements of instruments to evoke the changes of the seasons. Each season is represented by its own **concerto**. Beautiful violin solos bring to mind peaceful summer days. Groups of strings playing loudly and furiously sound like storms brewing.

Who did Vivaldi inspire?

Vivaldi is behind some of the earliest and most innovative concertos for the violin. The extent of his talent and influence did not become apparent until the twentieth century. Only then was he recognized as an inspiration for other great composers such as Haydn and Bach. Bach admired Vivaldi's violin concertos and went on to arrange some of them for the keyboard.

Where can you hear or find out more about Vivaldi?

The Four Seasons is regularly played by all kinds of orchestras so look out for performances in your local area. You might be lucky enough to catch a performance by candlelight.

Other pieces to listen to:

Gloria, RV. 589
6 Flute Concerti, Op. 10
Lute/Mandolin/Guitar Concerti
12 Violin Concerti Op. 3

'What strikes me most about *The Four Seasons* is how Vivaldi evokes such strong images in such a direct way. The fast passages bristle with energy, the melodies communicate with beauty and simplicity; and the huge contrasts in the music enhance the effect of this on the listener.'

Violinist Nigel Kennedy

weblinks

For more information about Vivaldi, go to
www.waylinks.co.uk/fav/composer

Johann Sebastian Bach | 1685-1750

The German composer Johann Sebastian Bach was a religious man whose faith in God was the inspiration for much of his work. Wolfgang Amadeus Mozart, the eighteenth century composer, once said of Bach: 'He is the father, and we his children.'

'The father' of classical music was born in Eisenach, Thuringia (now part of Germany) in 1685. He was orphaned before he was ten years old and raised by his brother who taught him to play the organ. Bach's family had been musicians for generations.

When he was 15, Bach joined the choir at St Michael's church in Lüneberg. Here he had the freedom to learn all about music. He studied the violin and began composing his own works. In 1704, at just 19, Bach became an organist at Arnstadt where he performed in the New Church and headed a boy's choir. During this time he wrote some of his first church **cantatas**.

From 1708 to 1717 Bach was organist to Duke Wilhelm Ernst of Weimar. These were creative years in which he composed some of his most stirring music for the organ, including

Bach once said that music should be: 'An agreeable harmony for the honour of God and the premissable [sic] delights of the soul.'

Music Quotations by David Watson (Chambers, 1991)

Passacaglia and Fugue in C Minor. In 1717 he was appointed music director to Prince Leopold of Anhalt in Cöthen. In the following years he created such masterpieces as The 'Brandenburg' Concertos and *The Well-Tempered Clavier*.

In 1723 Bach took up the position of cantor at St Thomas's, the famed German school of music in Leipzig. Though he often struggled with finances and fought with the city authorities, he remained at St Thomas's for the rest of his life. He also produced some of his most moving spiritual music here, including Mass in B Minor and the St John and St Matthew Passions.

Bach's final years were hampered by poor eyesight. In 1749 an operation on his eyes led to total blindness and he died in 1750. In his lifetime he was never famous and he was buried in Leipzig in an unmarked grave.

Questions

Why is Bach considered to be a serious musician?

Bach was driven by his deep religious feelings to create music. He is often described as a religious composer but perhaps only a quarter of his work was for the Church. Even so his work often sounds serious to our ears. He also didn't write operas or ballets, devoting himself to stirring instrumental music or choral work.

When did Bach become well known?

During his life Bach did not become well known outside his own country, and even then he was famous as a keyboard player rather than a composer. He was admired by Mozart and Beethoven but it wasn't until nearly 80 years after his death that he was truly recognized as a great composer. This turning point came in 1829 when Mendelssohn performed Bach's St Matthew Passion.

Where can you hear Bach's music or find out more about him?

In Germany they are very proud of Bach. Each year Leipzig hosts hundreds of musical events dedicated to his music. If you can't make it to Germany, then look out for recitals of Bach's work in your area.

'Bach belongs not to the past, but to the future - perhaps the near future.'

The nineteenth century Irish playwright, George Bernard Shaw

Other pieces to listen to:

Little Organ Book
Little Clavier Book
'Goldberg Variations'
Christmas Oratorio
Musical Offering

weblinks

For more information about Bach, go to
www.waylinks.co.uk/fav/composer

George Frideric Handel | 1685–1759

The German-English composer George Frideric Handel was born in the same year as Johann Sebastian Bach. The two men grew up less than a hundred miles apart yet they never met. While Bach never achieved fame beyond Germany in his own lifetime, Handel was very cosmopolitan and eventually settled in London.

Handel was born in 1685 in Halle, Saxony (now part of Germany). His father hated music. Handel practised in secret and by the time he was 11 he was already an accomplished organ player. He is pictured here as a young man composing music at his organ. At 17, Handel became organist of Halle Cathedral. Then, in 1702, he joined the Hamburg opera orchestra before living in Italy for four years. In Italy he learned how to compose operas and **oratorios**. Before long Handel was in demand.

In 1710 Handel was appointed court musician to the Elector of Hanover. In the same year he visited London and wrote the successful opera *Rinaldo*. Handel found himself torn between

> 'Whether I was in my body or out of my body as I wrote it I know not. God knows.'
>
> Handel talking about the 'Hallelujah Chorus' in the oratorio *Messiah*
> *Essays on Music* by Romain Rolland
> (*Chambers Biographical Dictionary*, 1991)

Hanover and London. In 1714, he finally made England his permanent home and became a favourite with King George I, and later royals, for whom he wrote 'Water Music'. For many years Handel's Italian operas appealed to the English gentry, and he became artistic director at the Royal Academy of Music in London.

Unfortunately, by 1728 Italian operas were going out of fashion and Handel almost went bankrupt. He bounced back with a new form of composition, the English oratorio. These were Bible stories set to orchestral music with grand choruses. Handel conducted the oratorio concerts and would often play the solo organ parts himself.

Handel was a very private man. He tended to overeat and grew very fat. In 1737 he suffered a stroke but he went on to produce some of his best works. In 1742 he wrote his masterpiece, *Messiah*. Then in 1749 he created his famous 'Music for the Royal Fireworks'.

In his later years Handel went blind. He died in 1759 and was given an honourable burial in London's Westminster Abbey.

Questions

Why is Handel's *Messiah* important?

Handel made oratorios popular in England in his own day but by Victorian times this kind of music was out of fashion. This means that many of his oratorios are rarely heard today. However, *Messiah* is still popular, especially the rousing 'Hallelujah Chorus'. When it was first performed in front of George II he was so impressed that he sprang to his feet when he heard the chorus. Ever since it has been the custom to stand during the chorus.

Where did Handel get his ideas?

In his lifetime Handel must have worked very hard because he left behind a great deal of music. However, part of his talent was being able to 'borrow' ideas from other musicians or even from himself. Sometimes, parts of music that appear in one of his works have been rearranged and used again in another work. Handel was hugely confident and a great wit. Once when he was asked why he had copied part of another composer's work he replied: 'It's much too good for him; he did not know what to do with it.'

Where can you hear Handel's music?

Just as Handel charmed people of eighteenth century Europe with his melodic music, he still works his magic on us today. His majestic and joyful instrumental *Arrival of the Queen of Sheba* is often played at weddings when the bride walks down the aisle. 'Music for the Royal Fireworks' is sometimes played at firework displays on special occasions. Here Handel uses a whole orchestra to express the beauty and wonder of the fireworks. His oboes, bassoons and kettledrums add atmosphere and bring even more sparkle to the fireworks.

Other pieces to listen to:

'Chandos Anthems'
Semele
Samson
Zadok the Priest
The Harmonious Blacksmith

'Handel is the greatest composer who ever lived. I would bare my head and kneel at his grave.'

Beethoven (1824)

weblinks

For more information about Handel, go to
www.waylinks.co.uk/fav/composer

Mozart | 1756-1791

The Austrian composer Wolfgang Amadeus Mozart created one of the largest and most impressive selection of works of any composer. Today his reputation is such that many people would argue he is the most gifted musician who has ever lived.

Mozart was born in Salzburg in 1756. His father was a violinist and composer who taught his children music from an early age. Mozart's sister, Anna Maria, played the harpsichord. Mozart could play the piano beautifully by the time he was four. He is pictured here rehearsing at the piano as a young boy. There seemed no end to his abilities and at the age of eight he had written his first **symphony**. At 14 he had written an opera. His father was so delighted with his children's talents that he took them on a European tour. By the time he was a teenager Mozart had already performed in Germany, France, England, Holland, Switzerland and Italy. He had played in the magnificent Court of Versailles in France and entertained King George III of England.

In 1781 Mozart was in his mid-twenties. He made Vienna in Austria his permanent home and was happily married to Constanze Weber. In the next years he began writing some of the best material of his career. He created operas such as *The Marriage of Figaro* and *Don*

'It is a very great mistake to suppose that my art has become so exceedingly easy to me. I assure you that there is scarcely anyone who has worked at the study of composition as I have. You could hardly mention any famous composer whose works I have not diligently and repeatedly studied throughout.'
Mozart talking about his talent for music.

The Oxford Junior Companion to Music by Percy A. Scholes (Oxford, 1954)

Giovanni. Despite his amazing ability to turn out masterpiece after masterpiece he never made much money and struggled to look after his wife and six children. It has been suggested that his childish behaviour made matters worse.

In his lifetime Mozart composed 21 operas, an estimated 40 symphonies, over 50 **concertos**, 27 string quartets, 17 piano **sonatas** as well as various orchestral pieces, chamber music and church music. In the final year of his life he wrote the opera *The Magic Flute*, as well as an unfinished requiem. He died in 1791 from typhus fever – he was just 36 years old. His wife Constanze scraped the money together for his funeral and he was laid to rest in a pauper's grave.

Questions

Why does Mozart's music move us?
Mozart's music has the ability to delight and touch us. His early works can be light and enchantingly beautiful. This contrasts with some of his later works, especially his piano concertos, where it is possible to hear the despair and anger caused by the difficulties in his personal life.

How did Mozart compose his music?
Mozart composed such a huge amount of music in his short life that it is hard to imagine that he had time to sleep! He certainly had unconventional ways of working. When he was composing the opera *Don Giovanni* he didn't write the overture until the evening before the first performance. It's believed that he stayed up all night working while Constanze read him fairytales. By the time he delivered the score the orchestra had no time to rehearse the music.

'There is no feeling – human or cosmic, no depth, no height the human spirit can reach that is not contained in Mozart's music.'
The pianist Lili Kraus
The Classic FM Guide to Classical Music by Jeremy Nicholas (Pavilion, 1996)

Where can you hear Mozart's music?
Mozart's music is so versatile and expressive that it has been used in many films and advertisements. In the film *Alien* you can hear *Eine Kleine Nachtmusik.* In *The Last Action Hero* and *Trading Places* there are bursts of music from the opera *The Marriage of Figaro.* But there is nothing like hearing his works performed live by musicians and singers. Mozart's most popular works are regularly performed up and down the country.

Other pieces to listen to:

Cosi fan tutte
Symphony No 41 in C 'Jupiter'
Piano Concerto in A (No 23)

weblinks

For more information about Mozart, go to
www.waylinks.co.uk/fav/composer

Ludwig van Beethoven | 1770-1827

The German composer Ludwig van Beethoven battled with depression and deafness to become one of the greatest pianists and composers of all time.

Born in Bonn in 1770, Beethoven was taught to play the harpsichord and violin by his father who dreamed of his son becoming the next Mozart. Lessons began when he was just four years old but his father was a cruel teacher. He drank too much and kept his son up all night practising, hitting him when he made mistakes.

By the time he was seven Beethoven was performing in public. When he was 12 he composed his first published work, then, at 14 he became deputy court organist for the Elector Maximilian Franz. Recognizing the young man's outstanding talents, the Elector sent Beethoven to Vienna in Austria in 1787 to receive proper training. Two years later Beethoven returned to Bonn to look after his brothers because his father had lost his job and his mother was dying.

By 1792 Beethoven returned to Vienna. His reputation as a fine pianist grew but in private he was tormented by the onset of deafness. Losing his hearing made him depressed but it

'From where do I get my ideas? I cannot say with certainty. They come uncalled, directly, indirectly. I could grasp them with my hands: in the open, from Nature, in the forest, in the quiet of the night, in the early morning. Sometimes moods which the poet expresses in words come to me in tones. They ring, storm, and roar until they finally stand before me in notes.'
Beethoven talking about how he composed his masterpieces.

also seemed to encourage great spurts of creativity. Beethoven's works can be divided into three distinct periods. Up until about 1800 he was influenced by classical composers such as Mozart and Haydn. In the following years he seemed to let go of tradition and allow his own creativity to take over. He produced epics like the *Eroica* symphony, his famous Symphony No 5 in C Minor and the *Appassionata* piano sonata.

Beethoven's final period began after 1818 when he had become totally deaf. By this time he lived in squalor and had become impossibly arrogant and irritable. Even so he composed such masterpieces as the *Hammerklavier* piano sonata and his famous Symphony No 9 in D. Beethoven continued to compose, conduct and play until his death in 1827. His final words are said to have been: 'I shall hear in heaven.'

Questions

What are Beethoven's first three symphonies like?

Beethoven composed nine great **symphonies** over 23 years. By listening to these works it is possible to chart the development of his style. The first two symphonies are influenced by the classical composers Haydn and Mozart and seem lighter and more traditional than the works that follow. When Beethoven wrote Symphony No 3 in E Flat, he was already going deaf. Yet, it is more expressive and emotional than the previous two works and is so innovative that it has been described as the 'greatest single step made by an individual composer in the history of music.'

What is special about his final symphonies?

Symphony No 5 in C Minor is a great favourite filled with contrasting movements of music. The 6th Symphony is often called the 'Pastoral' symphony. This time Beethoven sets his love of nature to music and there is a

wonderful interpretation of a storm in the country. The 9th Symphony is called his great 'Choral' symphony. It ends with a magnificent vocal chorus. It is powerful because Beethoven writes for voices as if they were musical instruments. It is amazing to think he achieved such beauty when he couldn't hear a note.

Where can you find out more about Beethoven?

It is possible to visit the house where Beethoven was born in Bonn, Germany. These days the house is a museum to the great composer.

Other pieces to listen to:

Sonata No 8 in C Minor 'Pathetique'
Sonata No 14 in C sharp Minor 'Moonlight'
Piano Concerto No 4 in G
Violin Concerto in D

'I have never seen an artist more concentrated, energetic and fervent.'

The German poet Johann Wolfgang von Goethe (1749-1832)

weblinks

For more information about Beethoven, go to
www.waylinks.co.uk/fav/composer

Felix Mendelssohn | 1809-1847

The composer Schumann once called Felix Mendelssohn 'the Mozart of the nineteenth century'. Like Mozart, Mendelssohn stunned people with his beautiful piano playing while he was still a child. He was also famous for composing music that expressed joy and happiness.

Born in 1809 to a rich family, Mendelssohn had a privileged and happy childhood. He grew up in Hamburg, Germany and together with his sister, Fanny, was taught to play the piano and violin by some of the best teachers of the day. Mendelssohn's talent shone from an early age and he made his first public appearance on the piano when he was ten. At 16 he had already written his Symphony in C Minor and the B Minor Quartet. A year later he created the overture *A Midsummer Night's Dream*. Some people thought he was even more talented than Mozart had been at the same age.

In 1829, aged just 20, he managed another amazing feat. He conducted a performance of Bach's St Matthew Passion. It was an ambitious project that revived interest in Bach who was not very popular at the time. In the same year Mendelssohn made the first of his ten trips to Britain. In time he became a great favourite of Queen Victoria.

'Though everything else may appear shallow and repulsive, even the smallest task in music is so absorbing, and carries us so far away from town, country, earth, and all worldly things, that it is truly a blessed gift of God.'

Mendelssohn talking about his love of music.

Luck seemed to follow Mendelssohn. On a personal level he was happily married and raised five children. Professionally he moved from one prestigious post to the next. He was musical director of the Leipzig Gewandhaus Orchestra and helped turn it into the best orchestra in the world. In 1840 the King of Prussia asked him to become a conductor and director of music to the court. Then, in 1843 he founded the famous music school in Leipzig. For one who lived such a charmed life, death came early. When his beloved sister, Fanny, died in 1847 he collapsed with grief. Six months later he also died – he was just 38 years old.

Questions

What is Mendelssohn's connection to Scotland?

One of Mendelssohn's best-known works is *The Hebrides* overture (also known as 'Fingal's Cave'). He visited Scotland in the summer of 1829 and was inspired by the cave near the Isle of Mull. The romantic overture expresses his emotions and evokes the waves of the sea as they lap the shoreline. Scotland was also the inspiration for his Symphony No 3 in A Minor, 'Scottish'.

Why is Mendelssohn called a 'Sunshine Composer'?

In life Mendelssohn was a friendly and happy person. Most of his work reflects his cheerful disposition. His Symphony No 4 in A, 'Italian', from 1833 was inspired by a holiday in Italy. Through beautifully flowing melodies, he manages to capture the romance and spirit of the Mediterranean country. However, the dramatic **oratorio** *Elijah* shows Mendelssohn could produce something much deeper.

Where can you hear Mendelssohn's music today?

Millions of newly wed couples walk down the aisle accompanied by 'The Wedding March'. This joyous piece of music is from Mendelssohn's incidental music for the play *A Midsummer Night's Dream*. It became fashionable after it was played at the wedding of Queen Victoria's daughter in 1858.

'…the unexpected death of the celebrated Felix Mendelssohn, has spread universal sorrow and commiseration throughout the musical community. It is on first recovering from a blow like the present, when we are unable to contemplate the void which a man leaves in his art… "Where shall we find this man's successor?" "How will music now fare?"'

Musical Times, January 1848

Other pieces to listen to:

Piano Concerto in G Minor
Symphony No 5 in D 'Reformation'
Violin Concerto in E Minor
Lieder ohne Worte (Songs Without Words), especially 'Spring Song'

weblinks

For more information about Mendelssohn, go to
www.waylinks.co.uk/fav/composer

Johannes Brahms | 1833-1897

The German composer Johannes Brahms came from such a poor family that when he was a boy he played the piano for money in inns and bars. He went on to become one of the most respected classical composers of his day.

Born in Hamburg in 1833, Brahms was the son of a double bass player who performed with the Hamburg Theatre Orchestra. Though times were hard, Brahms' father managed to scrape the money together to get his son a good piano teacher. The sacrifice paid off and by the time Brahms was ten he was performing classical music in public.

In 1853 Brahms set off on tour with the talented Hungarian violinist Eduard Remenyi. During his time away he met inspirational composers such as Franz Liszt and Robert Schumann. Brahms was already composing music and it was Schumann who recognized his early genius. He was so impressed by the young man's originality that he invited him to move in with him and his wife, Clara, with whom he became lifelong friends. Schumann also introduced him to the music publishers who eventually published his Piano Concerto No 1 in D Minor.

In his mid-twenties Brahms worked as court

musician to a German prince. In his spare time he composed but it wasn't until he moved to Vienna in around 1870 that he

'When I feel the urge to compose, I begin by appealing directly to my Maker and I first ask Him three most important questions pertaining to our life here in the world – whence, wherefore, whither.'
Brahms talking about how he composed his music.

Music All Around Me by A. Hopkins (Frewin, 1967)

started creating music for the orchestra. In 1873, his Variations on a Theme by Haydn brought him fame and financial security. He went on to write many kinds of music, including four **symphonies**, two piano **concertos**, a violin concerto, chamber music, organ music, waltzes and choral music. Brahms liked the quiet life. He never married. When he did become successful he chose to live simply. He is often likened to Beethoven, but this was as much for his bad-temper as his talent. He died in Vienna in 1897.

Questions

Why is Brahms like Beethoven?

Brahms had a traditional approach to music. He didn't have much time for contemporary musicians. Brahms was influenced by the great composers, especially Beethoven. His First Symphony has been called 'Beethoven's Tenth Symphony' (though there is evidence that Beethoven himself wrote an incomplete tenth symphony). This was by no means an insult; it was simply recognizing the strength of a suite of music that has also been called 'the greatest First Symphony in history'.

Did Brahms have a less serious side?

Playing light entertainment music for the customers of Hamburg's cafes and bars did seem to have some influence on Brahms' later work. He was a fan of the famous waltz composer Johann Strauss and he composed some waltzes of his own. Among his 16 Waltzes from 1865 are some of the most light-hearted and enjoyable waltzes of the time.

What inspired Brahms?

Brahms loved reading books. He once said: 'Whoever wishes to play well must not only practise hard but also read a great many books'. Strangely, this love of books never found its way into his work. He never wrote an opera or other work for the stage and he never set any literature to music.

'I felt…that one day there must suddenly emerge the one who would be chosen to express the most exalted spirit of the times in an ideal manner, one who would not bring us mastery in gradual developmental stages but who, like Minerva [Roman Goddess of War], would spring fully armed from the head of Jove [King of the Roman gods]. And he has arrived – a youth at whose cradle the graces and heroes of old stood guard. His name is Johannes Brahms.'

The composer, Robert Schumann
(*Neue Zeitschrift*, 1844)

Other pieces to listen to:

Symphony No 4 in E Minor
Piano Concerto No 1 in D Minor
21 Hungarian Dances
Tragic Overture
German Requiem

weblinks

For more information about Brahms, go to
www.waylinks.co.uk/fav/composer

Pyotr Tchaikovsky | 1840-1893

Best known for his romantic ballets and the stirring *1812 Overture*, Pyotr Ilyich Tchaikovsky is the most famous Russian composer of the nineteenth century.

Tchaikovsky was born in Kamsko-Votkinsk in Russia. When he was seven his father returned from St Petersburg with a beautiful musical box that played some of Mozart's works. The young boy was captivated by the music and began to learn the piano. The family moved to St Petersburg when Tchaikovsky was eight. Later, he began a career in the civil service but his love of music refused to go away. At 22 he left his job and began studying at the Conservatory in Moscow. By the time he was 26 his music was performed in public. Early successes included his Second Symphony ('Little Russian' symphony) and his Piano Concerto in B Flat Minor.

Throughout his life Tchaikovsky suffered terribly with anxiety and nervous illness. One of his many irrational fears was that his head would

'On my word of honour, I have never felt such self-satisfaction, such pride, such happiness, as in the knowledge that I have created a good thing.'

A letter from Tchaikovsky to P Jurgenson, August 1893
Chambers Biographical Dictionary
(Chambers, 1991)

fall off if he conducted an orchestra. As a result he didn't conduct any of his own music until he was 51. Another problem was his personal life. Though he married in 1877 he left his wife within a month of their wedding day. She suffered from a severe mental illness which he was unable to cope with. One of the most mysterious aspects of his life is the financial support that he received from a rich widow. For 11 years Nadezhda von Meck provided him with enough money to live in the countryside where he could compose in peace and quiet. Though Tchaikovsky wrote to Nadezhda regularly they only ever met once, and that was by accident.

The rich widow's support meant Tchaikovsky could devote himself to writing some of the most popular classical music to come out of Russia. Among his best works are six **symphonies** and five symphonic poems, as well as operas, ballets, chamber music and choral work. He died in 1893 in mysterious circumstances. For many years it was believed he died from cholera but more recently historians suggest that he committed suicide.

Questions

What makes Tchaikovsky so popular?
Tchaikovsky remains popular because he wrote music that expresses every emotion from happiness to terrible sadness. Pieces like *Capriccio Italien*, which was inspired by a visit to Italy, or the waltz from *Sleeping Beauty* are light and exciting. His *1812 Overture* is loud and brash. While his Symphony No 6 in B Minor ('Pathétique') is sad and moving. Tchaikovsky believed his Sixth Symphony was his best piece of work.

Why is *The Nutcracker* suite a great favourite?
Tchaikovsky wrote some of the most beautiful ballets, including *Swan Lake* and *Sleeping Beauty*. He wrote the ballet *The Nutcracker* suite near the end of his life in 1892. Since that time *The Nutcracker* has become one of the most popular ballets of all time, especially at Christmas. The story of the ballet is based on a fairytale in which a little girl has a magical dream on Christmas night. In her dream the girl is given a pair of nutcrackers that look like a strange little man. The adventures begin when he comes to life. Tchaikovsky wrote some of his most tuneful and delightful music for this ballet, including 'Dance of the Sugar Plum Fairy', 'Waltz of the Flowers' and 'Russian Dance'.

Where can you hear Tchaikovsky's music?
Tchaikovsky's works are regularly performed by orchestras all over the country. There are also frequent performances of his ballets, especially at Christmas.

Other pieces to listen to:

Romeo and Juliet Fantasy Overture
Eugene Onegin
Piano Concerto No 1 in B Flat Minor
Violin Concerto in D

'Tchaikovsky was excessively sensitive; modest and unassertive in his dealings with all, he was deeply appreciative of any interest shown in him or in his works.'

Leopold Auer, Hungarian violinist and teacher

weblinks

For more information about Tchaikovsky, go to
www.waylinks.co.uk/fav/composer

Sir Edward Elgar | 1857-1934

Sir Edward Elgar is often cited as the first English composer of orchestral music. He will be forever remembered for his *Pomp and Circumstance Marches*, which brought us the tune for 'Land of Hope and Glory'.

Elgar was born in 1857 in Broadheath, near Worcester. His father owned a music shop and played the organ for a local church. He inspired his son to play music and gave him his first organ lessons. By the time Elgar was 12 he was standing in for his father as organist at the church. Later he taught himself to play the piano, cello, double bass, bassoon, trombone and he received violin lessons. He left school at 15 to join a lawyer's practice but he left after a year to pursue his love of music.

For many years Elgar made a living teaching the piano and violin. He also played violin for

'One day in my childhood I happened to get hold of a copy of Beethoven's First Symphony…It was a revelation!…I had never seen anything like that. How romantic it all felt! I think it was this startling experience that first inspired me with a real passion for music.'
Elgar talking about the effect Beethoven had on his work.

The Oxford Junior Companion to Music by Percy A. Scholes (Oxford University Press, 1954)

a Birmingham orchestra, who performed some of his earliest compositions. He played the organ at the church and conducted a few bands. In 1889 he married Caroline Alice Roberts, one of his piano pupils. She came from a wealthy family and introduced him to influential people. In 1890 he gained some recognition for his *Overture Froissart.* From 1891 Elgar devoted himself to composing orchestral music. By 1899 he was being lauded as a musical genius for his masterpiece the *Enigma Variations.*

Elgar composed many orchestral works including two **symphonies**, **oratorios**, a violin **concerto**, music for marching bands, chamber music and songs. In 1904 he became the first British musician to have a three-day festival of his works performed in London. Shortly afterwards, he was knighted for his work.

Elgar lived until 1934 but the last 14 years of his life were quiet and he didn't compose any music. He had lost his wife in 1920 and the First World War had deeply affected his outlook on life. Nevertheless, he is remembered as an influential composer who put Britain on the map for music.

Questions

What is special about Elgar's music?
Many people like Elgar's music because it reminds them of Victorian England. His rousing marches are patriotic, while pieces like *Introduction* and *Allegro* capture the beauty of the English countryside.

Which other composers came from Britain?
In the seventeenth century Henry Purcell wrote keyboard music, choral works and operas. The contemporary of Elgar's, Gustav Holst, is remembered most for *The Planets*, the suite of music that brought us the tune to the hymn, 'I Vow to Thee My Country'. In the twentieth century Benjamin Britten wrote a variety of music, including his famous *The Young Person's Guide to the Orchestra* which introduces the listener to each instrument in the orchestra. Finally, there was Ralph Vaughan Williams whose Fantasia on 'Greensleeves' is based on the English folksong.

Other pieces to listen to:

Nimrod from the *Enigma Variations*
Symphony No 1 in A Flat
Cockaigne
Falstaff
Salut d'Amour

When Elgar died a close friend of his wrote:

'Eulogies pour in on every side, tributes to his genius, life and character, but he has written his own biography as no other man can ever do. He is our Shakespeare of music, born and died on the soil in the heart and soul of England with his love of his country, its music, and its meaning in his own heart and soul.'

weblinks

For more information about Elgar, go to
www.waylinks.co.uk/fav/composer

Other classic composers

There are many more composers' works for you to hear and get to know. Here are a few more introductions:

Franz Joseph Haydn (1732-1809)

Often called the 'father of the symphony' or 'father of the orchestra', the Austrian composer Joseph Haydn was alive at the same time as Mozart and Beethoven. He had a generous patron who encouraged him to compose music as well as give daily performances. This gave Haydn the chance to experiment so he tried many orchestral arrangements that hadn't been tried before. Mozart was a great fan of Haydn and dedicated some of his early works to the older man. Haydn admired Mozart and tried to promote his music. For a while Haydn was Beethoven's teacher though he didn't appreciate Beethoven's music in the same way as Mozart's. Considered to be a pioneer of orchestral music, some of Haydn's most famous works include his Symphony No 94 in G (the 'Surprise' symphony) and his choral works, *The Creation* and *The Seasons*.

Franz Peter Schubert (1797-1828)

The composer Franz Peter Schubert was born in Vienna, Austria. As a child he was a gifted violinist and pianist and played in an orchestra. By the time he was 17 he was a music teacher and had already begun composing music. He caught the public's eye in 1818 when his first overtures were performed in public. He was inspired by Beethoven who lived in Vienna at the same time. Though Schubert admired the older man and visited the coffee house which Beethoven regularly visited, they never actually spoke. Schubert died at just 31 but in his short lifetime he composed some of the most expressive music of the times. Conveying every emotion from happiness to sadness, his music is woven together with beautiful melodies. Popular works include Symphony No 8 in B Minor ('Unfinished') and *Rosamunde*.

Frédéric François Chopin (1810-1849)

Once called 'The poet of the piano', Frédéric François Chopin is one of the most popular composers of all time. Born in Poland, he eventually made Paris his home. It was here that his beautifully crafted and melodious piano pieces became fashionable. Never blessed with good health Chopin died when he was just 39 years old. He left behind a collection of miniatures or short works that all great pianists strive to play. Among his most beloved works are his *Nocturnes* or 'night pieces', which are like love poems set to music. His own favourite piece was the *Grande Valse Brillante* in A Minor. Other famous compositions include Waltz in D Flat (the 'Minute' waltz) and Fantasie in C Sharp Minor.

Robert Alexander Schumann (1810-1856)

The German composer Robert Schumann was alive at the same time as Mendelssohn and Chopin. He is mostly remembered for his Romantic music which is expressive and full of imaginative ideas. Born in Zwickau in Saxony (now part of Germany) in 1810, his parents were keen for him to become a lawyer but he was drawn towards music. He studied piano under Friedrich Wieck and published his first compositions while still in his early twenties. In 1830 he formed a close attachment to Wieck's daughter, Clara. She was much younger than him so they waited until 1840 to get married. Throughout his life he suffered terribly with his nerves and he attempted suicide on many occasions. He eventually died at the age of 46. By this time he was believed to be insane. Despite his personal difficulties, Schumann has left behind some of the most popular piano music, as well as four **symphonies**, chamber music and choral works. His most famous works include *Abegg* theme and variations, *Papillons* and 'Scenes from Childhood'.

Johann Strauss II (1825-1899)

The Austrian composer Johann Strauss II is also known as the 'The Waltz King'. Famous for his tuneful and entertaining music, he was much admired by Brahms, and other more serious classical composers. He was born in Vienna in 1825 and died there in 1899. He came from the great Strauss family of musicians – his father being Johann Strauss I, the well-known violinist, conductor and composer, and his brothers being Josef and Eduard, the conductors. Strauss II is particularly associated with waltzes and other dance music – he wrote 400 waltzes, including the well-known *The Blue Danube, Wine, Woman and Song* and *Tales from the Vienna Woods*; and the *Tritsch Tratsch* and *Thunder and Lightning* polkas. He also wrote some fine operattas like *The Bat* and *The Gypsy Baron*.

Sergei Sergeyevich Prokofiev (1891-1953)

The Russian composer Sergei Prokofiev first made a name for himself as a talented pianist. He later wrote piano concertos, symphonies, opera, ballet, choral works and musical scores for films. Many children know about him because he wrote the much-loved symphonic fairy tale *Peter and the Wolf*. For many young people this piece of music is an introduction to all the instruments in the orchestra.

Prokofiev was born in 1891 in Sontzovka in the Ukraine. He left Russia in 1918 for political reasons. First he moved to the USA, then to Paris, where he produced masterpieces such as his opera *The Love for Three Oranges* and the ballet *The Prodigal Son*. He never lost touch with his homeland and returned to Russia in 1932. Though artists were severely restricted by the government he managed to produce some of his greatest works at that time, including the ballets *Romeo and Juliet* and *Cinderella*; and the opera *War and Peace*.

Glossary

Concerto
A piece of music for an orchestra and one, or sometimes two or more, instrumental soloists. The part played by the solo instrument(s) contrasts with the music played by the orchestra.

Cantata
A piece of music for one or more solo voices accompanied by an orchestra or a smaller instrumental group. A choir may also be included.

Oratorio
A large-scale piece of music with a religious theme, usually for vocal soloists, choir and orchestra. An oratorio can be thought of as an opera without stage action or scenery.

Sonata
Originally a piece of music in three or four movements (sections) for one or more instruments or a small group. The term is now usually used to describe a piece of music for a single melody instrument, such as the violin, accompanied by the piano or another instrument that can play chords. Piano sonatas, however, are for the piano alone.

Symphony/Symphonies
A large-scale piece of orchestral music in several movements (sections). There are no solo instruments as in a concerto, although individual members of the orchestra may have short solo parts within the symphony.

Index